# Africa

## by Mike Graf

Consultant:
Colleen Keen
Geography Department
Gustavus Adolphus College
St. Peter, Minnesota

Bridgestone Books
an imprint of Capstone Press
Mankato, Minnesota

Bridgestone Books are published by Capstone Press
151 Good Counsel Drive, P.O. Box 669, Mankato, Minnesota 56002
http://www.capstone-press.com

*Library of Congress Cataloging-in-Publication Data*
Graf, Mike.
    Africa/by Mike Graf.
    p.cm.—(Continents)
    Summary: An introduction to the geography, various regions, natural resources,
people, and wildlife of Africa, the world's second largest continent.
    Includes bibliographical references and index.
    ISBN-0-7368-1414-0 (hardcover)
    1. Africa—Juvenile literature. [1. Africa] I. Title. II. Continents (Mankato, Minn.)
DT3 .G69 2003
916—dc21
                                            2001008427

**Editorial Credits**
Erika Mikkelson, editor; Karen Risch, product planning editor; Linda Clavel, designer and
    illustrator; Image Select International, photo researchers

**Photo Credits**
Art Directors and TRIP/M. Jelliffe, 15, 22 (Serengeti); J. Sweeney, 17
Betty Press/Woodfin Camp/PictureQuest, 20
Corbis/Roger Wood, 11; Peter Johnson, 19
Digital Stock, 22 (Pyramids)
Digital Wisdom/Mountain High, cover
Eyewire, 13, 22 (Mount Kilimanjaro)
Robert Caputo/Stock Boston Inc./PictureQuest, 21

1 2 3 4 5 6 07 06 05 04 03 02

# Table of Contents

# Fast Facts about Africa

**Population:** 794 million (early 2000s estimate)

**Number of countries:** 53

**Largest cities:** Cairo, Egypt; Lagos, Nigeria; Kinshasa, Democratic Republic of the Congo

**Longest river:** Nile River, 4,160 miles (6,695 kilometers)

**Highest point:** Mount Kilimanjaro, 19,341 feet (5,895 meters) above sea level

**Lowest point:** Lake Assal, 509 feet (155 meters) below sea level

# Countries in Africa

1. Morocco
2. Western Sahara
3. Mauritania
4. Senegal
5. The Gambia
6. Guinea-Bissau
7. Guinea
8. Sierra Leone
9. Liberia
10. Tunisia
11. Algeria
12. Mali
13. Burkina Faso
14. Ivory Coast
15. Ghana
16. Togo
17. São Tomé and Príncipe
18. Benin
19. Niger
20. Libya
21. Egypt
22. Nigeria
23. Chad
24. Cameroon
25. Equatorial Guinea
26. Gabon
27. Republic of the Congo
28. Central African Republic
29. Sudan
30. Eritrea
31. Djibouti
32. Ethiopia
33. Somalia
34. Kenya
35. Uganda
36. Rwanda
37. Burundi
38. Democratic Republic of the Congo
39. Tanzania
40. Angola
41. Zambia
42. Malawi
43. Namibia
44. Botswana
45. Zimbabwe
46. Mozambique
47. South Africa
48. Lesotho
49. Swaziland
50. Comoros
51. Seychelles
52. Madagascar
53. Mauritius

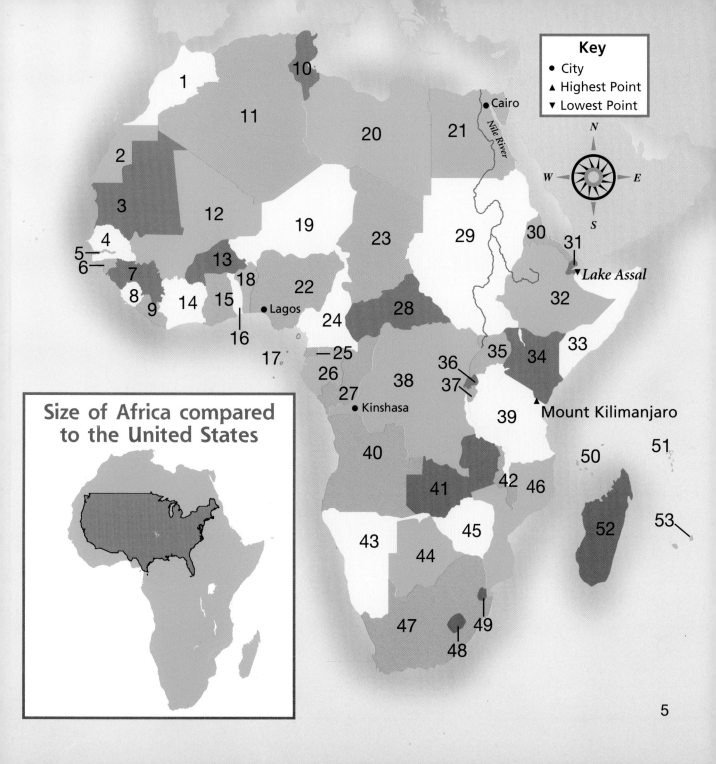

## Key
- ● City
- ▲ Highest Point
- ▼ Lowest Point

N
W E
S

1

10

11

2

3

12

4

5

6

7

13

18

8

14

15

9

16

22

● Lagos

17

24

25

26

27

● Kinshasa

20

21

Nile River

● Cairo

23

29

30

31

▼ Lake Assal

32

33

28

34

35

36

37

38

39

▲ Mount Kilimanjaro

40

41

42

46

45

43

44

47

48

49

50

51

52

53

**Size of Africa compared to the United States**

5

# Africa

Africa is the second largest continent. The Atlantic Ocean lies west of Africa. The Indian Ocean is to the east. The Mediterranean Sea lies to the north. The Red Sea is northeast of Africa.

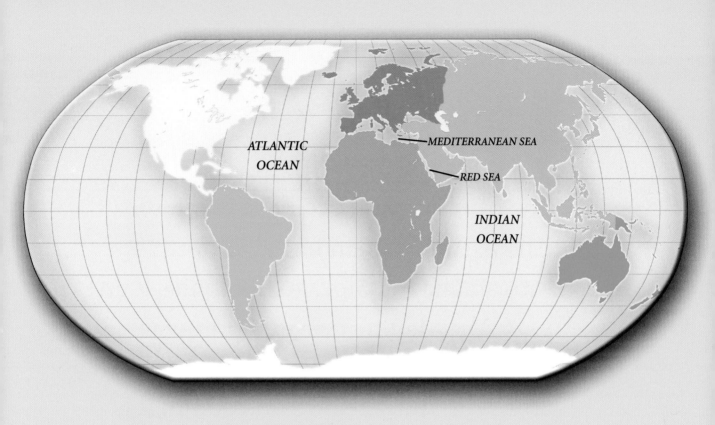

ATLANTIC
OCEAN

MEDITERRANEAN SEA

RED SEA

INDIAN
OCEAN

**Key**

Africa

Antarctica

Asia

Australia

Europe

North America

South America

# Africa's Land

The equator runs through the middle of Africa. Africa stretches as far north of the equator as it does to the south. Rain forests grow near the equator. Savannas and deserts lie north and south of the rain forests. In the far north and south, it is wet in the winter and dry in the summer.

**equator**

an imaginary line around the middle of Earth

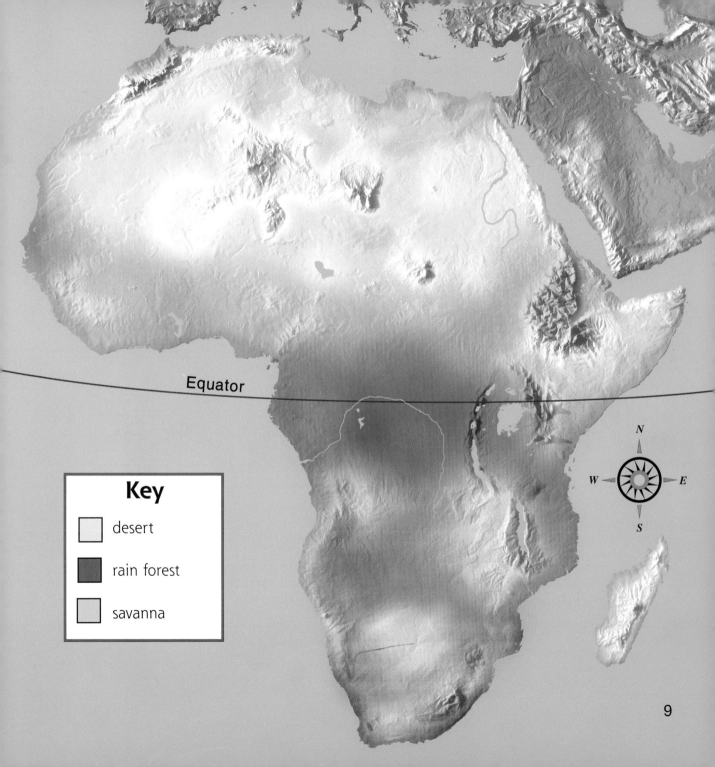

Equator

**Key**

desert

rain forest

savanna

N
W    E
S

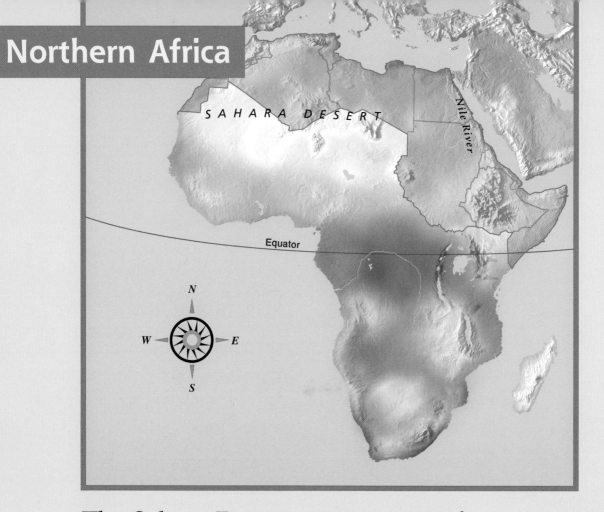

The Sahara Desert covers most of
northern Africa. It is the largest hot
desert in the world.

**Nile River**

The Nile River flows through northeast
Africa. People have lived along the Nile
in Egypt for thousands of years.

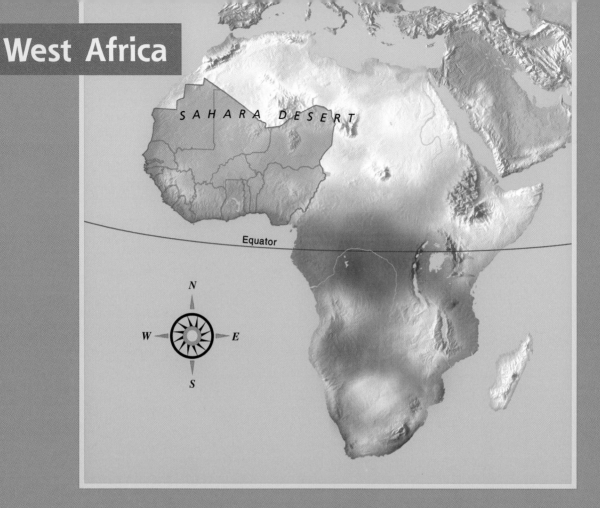

West Africa has deserts, savannas, and rain forests. The Sahara Desert covers the northern part of this region.

**region**
a large area of
land or water

**African elephants**

Savannas lie in the central part of this region. Elephants and giraffes live on the savanna. Rain forests cover the southern parts of West Africa.

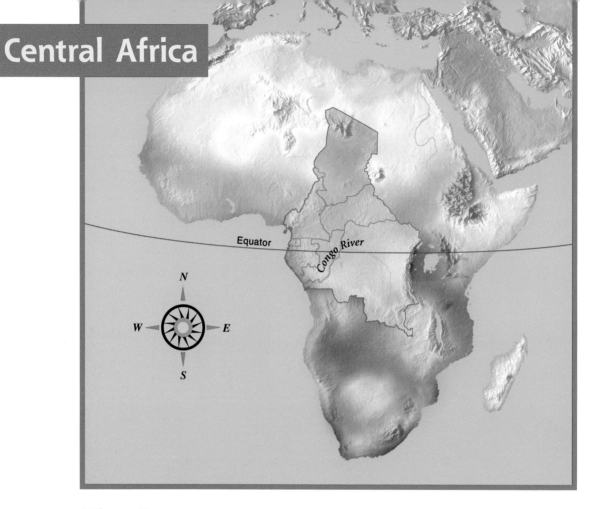

The Congo Basin is an area in central Africa. The Congo River flows through the basin. Farmers there grow peanuts and coffee beans.

gorilla

Rain forests cover much of central Africa. Animals such as monkeys and gorillas live in the rain forests.

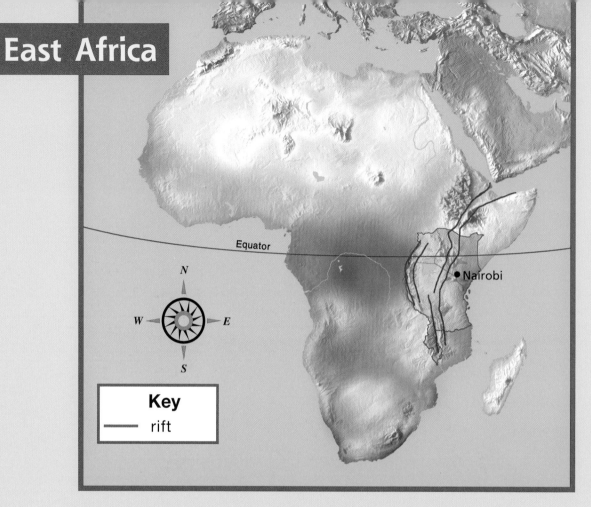

Equator

**Key**
— rift

• Nairobi

The Great Rift Valley lies in East Africa.
Cracks in Earth's crust made this 3,750-mile
(6,035-kilometer) valley.

Nairobi is in Kenya. It is one of Africa's largest cities. The city has many tall, modern buildings.

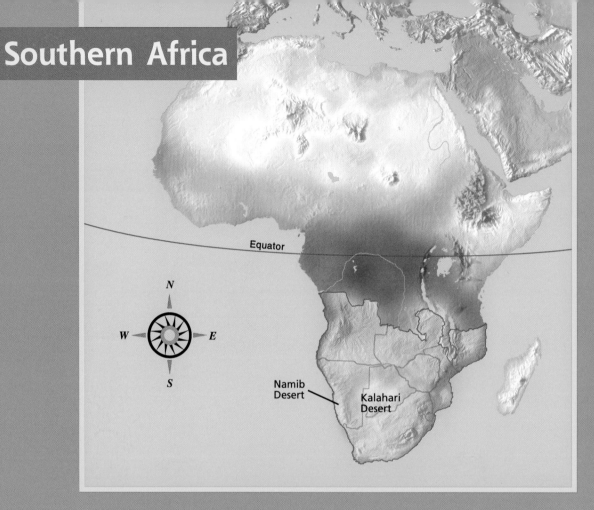

Equator

N
W — E
S

Namib
Desert

Kalahari
Desert

Southern Africa has important minerals.
People mine diamonds and gold there.
Farmers grow corn, wheat, and fruit.

Namib Desert

The Namib Desert lies along the coast of Namibia. The Kalahari Desert lies in the central part of southern Africa.

# Africa's People

farmers in Kenya

Many people in Africa live in small villages. They grow food to feed their families. They may sell their extra food at markets.

Cairo, Egypt

Millions of Africans live in cities. Cairo,
Egypt, and Johannesburg, South Africa,
are two large cities in Africa.

# Reading Maps: Africa's Sights to See

1. People built the Great Pyramids about 5,000 years ago. Look at the maps on pages 5 and 7. In what country are the pyramids found? Is this country north or south of the Mediterranean Sea?

2. Mount Kilimanjaro is Africa's highest mountain. The mountain is so high that snow and ice cover its peak year-round. Look at the map on page 7. What ocean lies to the east of Mount Kilimanjaro?

3. The Serengeti Plain is home to millions of African animals. Tourists from all over the world come to see the wildlife there. Look at the map on page 5. Which direction would you go to get to Cairo, Egypt, from the Serengeti?

# Words to Know

**continent** (KON-tuh-nuhnt)—one of the seven main landmasses of Earth

**desert** (DEZ-urt)—a very dry area of land; deserts may be hot like the Sahara or cold like the desert in Antarctica.

**equator** (e-KWAY-tur)—an imaginary line around the middle of Earth; regions near the equator usually are warm and wet.

**mine** (MINE)—to remove gold, diamond, copper, or other minerals from the ground

**rain forest** (RAYN FOR-ist)—a forest of tall trees that grows where the weather is warm and rainy all year

**rift** (RIFT)—a crack in the earth's surface

**savanna** (suh-VAN-uh)—a flat, grassy area with few or no trees

# Read More

**Foster, Leila Merrell.** *Africa.* Continents. Chicago: Heinemann Library, 2001.

**Fowler, Allan.** *Africa.* Rookie Read-About Geography. New York: Children's Press, 2001.

**Petersen, David**. *Africa.* A True Book. New York: Children's Press, 1998.

# Internet Sites

**Africa Information Center**
http://www.hmnet.com/africa/1africa.html
**ZoomSchool Africa: Africa's Geography**
http://www.enchantedlearning.com/school/Africa

# Index